What Animal Has These Parts?

EARS

AMY CULLIFORD

A Crabtree Roots Book

CRABTREE
Publishing Company
www.crabtreebooks.com

School-to-Home Support for Caregivers and Teachers

This book helps children grow by letting them practice reading. Here are a few guiding questions to help the reader with building his or her comprehension skills. Possible answers appear here in red.

Before Reading:

• What do I think this book is about?
  - *I think this book is about ears.*
  - *I think this book is about animals that have ears.*

• What do I want to learn about this topic?
  - *I want to learn which animal has the biggest ears in the world.*
  - *I want to learn why animals have ears.*

During Reading:

• I wonder why...
  - *I wonder why some ears are hairy.*
  - *I wonder why ears are different sizes.*

• What have I learned so far?
  - *I have learned that elephants have big ears.*
  - *I have learned that ears can be many different shapes.*

After Reading:

• What details did I learn about this topic?
  - *I have learned that animal ears can be different colors.*
  - *I have learned that big animals usually have big ears.*

• Read the book again and look for the vocabulary words.
  - *I see the word **ears** on page 3 and the word **hamster** on page 4. The other vocabulary words are found on page 14.*

What **animal** has
these little **ears**?

A **hamster!**

Which animal has these big ears?

An **elephant**!

What animal has these black-and-white ears?

A **zebra**!

Word List

Sight Words

a	black	what
an	has	which
and	little	white
big	these	

Words to Know

animal

ears

elephant

hamster

zebra

26 Words

What **animal** has these little **ears**?

A **hamster**!

Which animal has these big ears?

An **elephant**!

What animal has these black-and-white ears?

A **zebra**!

What Animal Has These Parts?

Written by: Amy Culliford

Designed by: Bobbie Houser

Series Development: James Earley

Proofreader: Janine Deschenes

Educational Consultant: Marie Lemke M.Ed.

Photographs:

Shutterstock: Ercan Uc: cover; Tami Freed: p. 1;
stock_shot: p. 3, 5, 14; Nora Yusuf: p. 7, 14; Isabelle
OHara: p. 8-9, 14; Plum Photography: p. 10;
NaturesMomentsuk: p. 13-14

Library and Archives Canada Cataloguing in Publication

CIP available at Library and Archives Canada

Library of Congress Cataloging-in-Publication Data

CIP available at Library of Congress

Crabtree Publishing Company

www.crabtreebooks.com   1-800-387-7650

Published in the United States
Crabtree Publishing
347 Fifth Avenue, Suite 1402-145
New York, NY, 10016

Published in Canada
Crabtree Publishing
616 Welland Ave.
St. Catharines, ON, L2M 5V6